The Life-Changing Magic of Tidying Up:

The Japanese Art of Decluttering and Organizing

Summary

Contents

Introduction 8

I. Why can't I keep my house in order? 9

You can't tidy if you've never learned how 9

A tidying marathon doesn't cause rebound ...10

Tidy a little a day and you'll be tidying forever
....11

Why you should aim for perfection................12

The moment you start you reset your life 13

Storage experts are hoarders...........................14

Sort by category, not by location 15

Don't change the method to suit your
personality 15

Make tidying a special event, not a daily chore
....16

II. Finish discarding first 18

Start by discarding, all at once, intensely and
completely..18

Before you start, visualize your destination...19

Selection criterion: does it spark joy? 20

One category at a time 20

Starting with mementos spell certain failure.21

Don't let your family see 22

If you're mad at your family, your room may be the cause 23

What you don't need, your family doesn't either 24

Tidying is a dialogue with one's self 25

What to do when you can't throw something away...25

III. Tidying by category works like magic **27**

Tidying order: Follow the correct order of categories...27

Clothing: Place every item of clothing in the house on the floor 28

Loungewear: Downgrading to "loungewear" is taboo..29

Clothing storage: Fold it right and solve your storage problems...30

How to fold: The best way to fold for perfect appearance...31

Arranging clothes: The secret to energizing your closet 32

Storing socks: Treat your socks and stockings with respect 33

Seasonal clothes: Eliminate the need to store off-season clothes...33

Storing books: Put all your books on the floor 34

Unread books: "Sometime" means "never" ...35

Books to keep: Those that belong in the hall of fame 36

Sorting papers: Rule of thumb—discard everything...36

All about papers: How to organize troublesome papers...38

Komono (miscellaneous items): Keep things because you love them—not "just because"...39

Common types of *komono: Disposables* 41

Small change: Make "into my wallet" your motto 42

Sentimental items: Your parents' home is not a haven for mementos..43

Photos: Cherish who you are now 43

Astounding stockpiles I have seen.................44

Reduce until you reach the point where something clicks...44

Follow your intuition and all will be well 45

IV. Storing your things to make your life shine 46

Designate a place for each thing 46

Discard first, store later 47

Storage: pursue ultimate simplicity 48

Don't scatter storage spaces 48

Forget about "flow planning" and "frequency of use"...49

Never pile things: vertical storage is the key .50

No need for commercial storage items 51

The best way to store bags is in another bag .52

Empty your bag every day 53

Items that usurp floor space belong in the closet 54

Keep things out of the bath and the kitchen sink 55

Make the top shelf of the bookcase your personal shrine 55

Decorate your closet with your secret delights 56

Unpack and de-tag new clothes immediately 57

Don't underestimate the "noise" of written information 58

Appreciate your possessions and gain strong allies...58

V. The magic of tidying dramatically transforms your life 60

Put your house in order and discover what you really want to do..60

The magic effect of tidying............................60

Gaining confidence in life through the magic of tidying 61

An attachment to the past or anxiety about the future 62

Learning that you can do without..................65

Do you greet your house? 66

Your possessions want to help you 67

Your living space affects your body 68

Is it true that tidying increases good fortune?
....69

How to identify what is truly precious...........69

Being surrounded by things that spark joy
makes you happy...70

Your real life begins after putting your house
in order..71

Millionaire Mind Book Summaries 73

Introduction

This #1 *New York Times* best-selling guide to tidying and decluttering your home from Japanese cleaning consultant Marie Kondo will take you step-by-step through her revolutionary *KonMari* Method for organizing, storing, and simplifying, which will turn your home into a permanently clean and clutter-free space.

The key to successful tidying is to tackle your house in the correct order, to keep only the things that bring you joy and to do it all at once, quickly and effectively.

The *KonMari* Method will not only transform your home; once you have your whole house in order, your whole life will change for the better. You will be more confident, more focused and less distracted, and you will have the courage to break free from the past and move on from the negative aspects of your life.

This summary highlights key ideas and captures important lessons found in the original book. Unessential information has been removed to save the reader time. If you've already read the original, this summary will serve as a reminder of main ideas and key concepts. If you haven't, don't worry, here you will find every bit of practical information without having to use so much time to read the original book.

I. Why can't I keep my house in order?

You can't tidy if you've never learned how

Most people assume that tidying skills come naturally. They spend time and money in order to learn various skills (e.g. cooking, sewing, dancing, etc.). But when it comes to tidying, they assume that they don't have to learn anything.

Remember your childhood days. Your parents scolded you when you didn't tidy up your room. But it is likely that they didn't teach you how to do the said task. This is a typical situation. You have to tidy up the place, but you don't know exactly what to do. Thus, you (and most of the people on this planet) are self-taught in the art of tidying.

Instruction in tidying is neglected not only at home, but also at school. Activities in home economics class usually focus on cooking (e.g. making hamburgers) and sewing (e.g. making aprons). Teachers play down the topic of tidying so they can discuss "more important" lessons. In most cases, tidying lessons consist of writing or reading some instructional paragraphs.

Food, shelter, and clothing are the most basic human needs, so you would think that where we live would be considered just as important as what we eat and what we wear. Yet in most societies, tidying - the task that keeps a home livable - is often disregarded because of the misconception that the ability to tidy is acquired through experience and therefore doesn't require training.

You can't be good at tidying if you don't know how to do it properly. Fortunately, it is not too late. This book will teach you the most important tricks, techniques, and strategies of tidying, and you will finally be able to escape the vicious cycle of clutter.

A tidying marathon doesn't cause rebound

Magazine columnists claim that rebound occurs if you'll clean your house in just one go. Some areas will be messy again in a short period of time. This assumption is wrong, though. You can clean an entire place without experiencing any rebound. If you will use the right technique, that is.

Your room will change drastically once you begin moving furniture around and getting rid of garbage. A rebound will occur only if you mistakenly believe that you have completed the tidying up process, when in fact you have only sorted and stored things halfway. By arranging your things and cleaning your place properly, you can maintain tidiness. If you put your house in order properly, you'll be easily able to keep it tidy, even if you are lazy or sloppy by nature.

Tidy a little a day and you'll be tidying forever

It's a good idea to clean a place in one fell swoop. The rebound that many people fear won't happen if you will use the right approach. What about cleaning a place bit by bit? Well, it turns out that the "slowly-but-surely" approach doesn't work in the art of tidying. If you will do the cleanup little by little, it will take you forever to finish the task. Make sure that you are getting significant results while tidying up your place.

Tidying gives you noticeable results. If your place is tidy, you can be sure that it is tidy. No "ifs" or "buts". To succeed in tidying, avoid dividing the task into bite sizes. Rather, clean up the place in one go. This "one shot" approach can change how you think about tidying. And once your mindset has changed, you will have an easier time developing new habits.

Important Note: Gradual tidying gives minimal results. Thus, you won't immediately see the benefits of your work. By going "all in", on the other hand, you can keep your place clutter-free and develop the right mindset.

Why you should aim for perfection

Perfection is said to be unattainable. That's why many people satisfy themselves with slow and/or inappropriate tidying approaches. Some people even limit themselves to one disposed item per day. They believe that this is enough since they would have disposed 365 items every year.

The main problem with this approach is that it encourages you to keep items you don't need. For example, if you have old notebooks, you might be tempted to keep one of them so you will have something to throw away tomorrow. Also, this approach will only work if you are buying one thing per day (which is impossible). Since the inflow of items is generally higher than the outflow, you will still end up with a lot of useless stuff.

The best way to tidy up your place is by doing it to the best of your ability. If you don't have the perseverance or diligence to do it regularly, aim for a "perfect tidying" at least once. You can make perfection more attainable using two techniques. First, check each item one by one and decide whether you should throw it away or not. And second, if you want to keep it, think about the best place for it.

The moment you start you reset your life

Many people have a tendency to tidy up their place before a stressful event (e.g. an exam). They search for unimportant documents and put them in a trash bin. Then, they will arrange their pens, papers, books, and other materials. Several hours will be spent on these activities. The crucial task (e.g. reviewing for an upcoming exam) will be completely forgotten until it stares at you in the face.

This usually results from people's tendency to procrastinate. They don't really want to organize their area. Reviewing for an exam is difficult, so they will focus on easier tasks first (e.g. arranging the pens on the table). In almost all cases, the need to organize will disappear once the real issue (e.g. the exam) is over. The person's life will return to normal.

However, keeping your room tidy all the time will help you focus on the most important tasks. Your mind won't be distracted by the clutter, so it will be forced to tackle the real issue. Don't use tidying as an excuse to delay important activities.

Storage experts are hoarders

Many problems arise when you are tidying up a place. But one of the most typical issues is storage. Many people spend a lot of time thinking where to store what. However, you shouldn't pay too much attention to this aspect. Keep in mind that features on how to organize and store your possessions and convenient storage products are usually accompanied by confusing and/or misleading taglines that make it sound simple (e.g. "make tidying fast and easy", "organize your place in no time"). These products claim to offer quick and easy ways that tempt many people, but they are just a superficial solution. They cannot directly solve clutter-related problems. Instead of getting rid of the garbage, you only end up hiding it.

A room can still be messy, even if it contains numerous drawers, shelves, racks, and other types of storage devices. The solution is not about buying the best storage products. Rather, it is in storing only the items that you actually need. Putting stuff away makes you feel that you have tidied up your place, but the problem will reappear once your storage devices become full.

Important Note: Do not store something that you don't need anymore. It will only lead to clutter. If you keep useless things, clutter won't disappear regardless of how many storage units you have.

Sort by category, not by location

Many people base their tidying efforts on a specific location. For example, they'll work on the kitchen today, the bathroom tomorrow, then the living room, the bedroom, etc. This approach, although logical, is ineffective. That's because it forces you to repeat your work many times.

It would be better if you'll sort your things by category. For instance, you can organize the books today, clothes tomorrow, etc. This way, you will know whether you have too much of anything. Excess stuff leads to clutter, but the category-based approach will help you get rid of it and maintain the tidiness of your home.

Don't change the method to suit your personality

Some organizing consultants claim that personality affects the causes of clutter. They also encourage people to choose or modify organizing methods to match their personality. This belief totally makes sense. If you are a lazy person, you should use an organizing approach made for lazy people, right? Well, no.

Choosing an approach based on your personality doesn't offer any significant benefit. People are generally busy and/or lazy. And they differ in terms of the things they like and dislike. Clearly, you shouldn't waste time in finding the "right" organizing approach.

It is likely that you belong to the "can't-keep-it, can't-throw-it-away" type. In fact, most people are of this type. The remaining minority belongs to the "can't-keep-it" category, and this is what you should actually aim for.

The main point here is that you shouldn't worry about your personality type. Don't change any aspect of the tidying approach contained in this book just to make it more appealing or convenient. You will just end up reducing its effectiveness. To tidy up your home effectively, you just have to focus on two actions: (1) discarding, and (2) choosing where to keep the things that you actually need. And you should always perform the "discarding" first.

Make tidying a special event, not a daily chore

For many people, organizing things is repetitive and endless, but that's because they falsely believe that they have to do it every day. You don't have to perform overall tidying every day. Rather, consider tidying as a special event that occurs once every few years. For some people, this event can even be once-in-a-lifetime.

Tidying can be divided into two types: (1) daily, and (2) special event. The daily type (e.g. returning something to its place after using it) will always be more or less necessary. But this book is all about the second type of tidying.

Once you have conducted the special type of tidying, you will have an orderly home and a much better lifestyle. You will get rid of the things you don't need. Conversely, tidying excessively on a daily basis can make you lose your interest in keeping things organized. The benefits you'll get are not enough to justify the effort required.

Important Note: Tidying your place means you will deal with many objects. And you can easily move or throw away useless objects. In fact, anyone can do it. Discard everything you don't need and organize your important stuff. Once the things you need are in their best place, you can congratulate yourself. You have accomplished a once-in-a-lifetime event called special tidying, and from now on, your life is going to be so much better.

II. Finish discarding first

Start by discarding, all at once, intensely and completely

Many people think they have tidied everything perfectly, only to notice that the clutter quickly returns. As time goes by, they keep collecting things that slowly begin to accumulate in their rooms, and before they know it, their entire home will be back to its former state. This is the rebound effect that many people fear. And, it occurs because the tidying process is incomplete. As mentioned earlier, the only way to overcome this is by organizing your place in one shot and breaking the habit of keeping useless things.

To get the best results, you must follow the proper order of tidying activities. Remember that there are only two activities here: discarding and storing things. The rule is simple: do not move on to the second task until you're sure that the first one is complete. In other words, do not store anything until you have disposed of everything you don't need, until you have thrown away all the useless stuff. Disobeying this rule can lead to failure.

Before you start, visualize your destination

At this point, the reason why you should discard things should be clear to you. However, do not throw away anything without any clear objective or plan. That means you should start the tidying up process by setting a goal. You surely have a reason for reading this book. Identify the motivation behind your desire to organize your place. List down the things you want to accomplish. Visualize the lifestyle you want to have after organizing your stuff. Don't settle for general goals such as "store away things" or "have a clutter-free life". Vivid and specific terms can help you maintain your motivation.

After visualizing your goal and describing it in concrete terms, can you go ahead and discard your stuff? No, don't do it yet. The best way to avoid rebounds is by going through each step of the process. The second step is all about determining the reason behind your goal. What are the most promising aspects of your desired lifestyle? Then, determine the reason behind your reason. For example, if you want to have a clutter-free life to avoid distractions, why do you dislike distractions? This multi-level analysis will help you identify your real needs and wants.

Selection criterion: does it spark joy?

There are many criteria that you can use when choosing what to throw away. For instance, you can discard an item once it is no longer useful (e.g. when it is damaged beyond repair). Or you may discard items that are outdated (e.g. stuff that is related to a past event). Discarding something is easy if you have a clear reason for your action. But it becomes extremely hard when you have no reason to throw it away.

Don't choose things that you should get rid of. Focusing on what to discard is a mistake in itself. Rather, choose the things you would like to keep. This approach makes the selection more enjoyable. The best way to do this is by taking each item in your hands and answering the simple question: "Does this spark joy?" If your answer is yes, keep it; otherwise, put it in the trash bin.

Important Note: Choose the items that give you joy. Then discard the items that don't.

One category at a time

Now that you know what you want to keep, you may start eliminating the unnecessary stuff. But how are you going to do this? It is best to base your tidying efforts on item categories. Do not organize your place by location. For example, it is ineffective to say: "I'll work on the home office first before proceeding to the living room". That's because some items may be stored in many different places. When you think you're done throwing away useless papers, you may find some more in other rooms. This unnecessary repetition of tasks can drain your motivation quickly.

Here is a step-by-step process that you can use:

1. Divide your items into categories.
2. Get all the items that belong to those categories. For example, collect all the clothes in your house and put them in one place.
3. Hold each outfit and decide whether you want to keep it or not. Do this for all the items you'll find. If a category has many different items, you may divide it into subcategories (e.g. bathroom products -> hair products, skincare products, grooming products, and so on.)

Starting with mementos spell certain failure

The degree of difficulty involved in deciding what to keep and what to discard varies depending on the category. Many people tend to get stuck halfway through the process because they start with mementos, with things that are particularly important to them. Things that trigger feelings and memories, such as photos, are not the place for beginners to start. Not only is the sheer volume of such items usually greater than those from any other category, but it is also much harder to decide whether or not to keep them. Therefore, it is best to start the selection process with unimportant item categories. The best sequence should be something like this: clothes first, then books, papers, miscellaneous items, and lastly, mementos.

When evaluating an item, do not limit yourself to its monetary value. You should also consider its function, the information it contains, and the memories attached to it.

Important Note: The process will be faster and easier if you will start with items you can easily throw away. The momentum that you build as you throw away unimportant things will improve your ability to make decisions once you reach the important stuff.

Don't let your family see

While organizing your room, you will surely have one or more heaps of garbage. This period is highly sensitive: things will go wrong if your parents or loved ones see what you are doing.

Tidying is good - there's nothing shameful about it. But hide it from your family because it is often hard for them to see you discard items. Just looking at large piles of stuff you're planning to throw away can make them anxious. They might think that some of those items might be useful to you in the future. Or they might want to keep a particular item since they gave it to you (e.g. souvenirs).

Your family will get your garbage from you in order to keep it. It doesn't matter whether they like the item or not. The mere act of thinking about throwing away an item can be painful for them. For instance, it is not uncommon for a mother to save her children's clothes from the garbage truck, even if there's no way that she could actually wear them.

If you're mad at your family, your room may be the cause

As you organize your stuff, you will surely notice your family's clutter. Tidying up your room is often not enough, and you may feel compelled to organize every part of the house in order to achieve your ideal lifestyle. Useless items will catch your attention, and you'll want to throw them away. But no matter what you do, don't throw away other people's stuff without their permission.

When you spend time cleaning other parts of the house, you will likely miss some garbage in your own room. So, you should mainly focus on keeping your own room clean and tidy. Throw away everything you don't need anymore. If you'll do it properly, your family will notice the changes (and the attendant benefits), and they will likely start to organize their own things.

Important Note: Never discard anything without asking for the owner's permission. The tidiness that you'll enjoy is not enough to justify the problems you may face once they find out what you did.

What you don't need, your family doesn't either

Younger people tend to have more things to discard than their older siblings. This is easy to understand: younger children tend to have many hand-me-down items. This tendency arises from two major reasons: (1) throwing away other people's gifts is hard, and (2) young people are not sure of what they want. Since they receive so many items from others, they don't really need to shop and therefore they don't really have the opportunity to develop the instinct for what truly inspires joy.

Giving things to other people can be a great idea, though. It is economical - the recipient won't have to spend money to get new stuff. In addition, seeing others appreciate your items can give you great happiness. However, you should never force your friends or family members to take your old things. Don't treat them as a way to keep things you don't want to throw away. Find out in advance what they actually like, and if you find something that fits the criteria, then and only then should you give it to them.

Tidying is a dialogue with one's self

Organizing your stuff can be a powerful recreational activity. In fact, many people consider tidying up as a form of meditation. While doing it, many of your worries will disappear. The work of carefully considering each item you own to see if it brings you joy requires a certain level of introspection.

To make excellent evaluations about your life, organize your things in a quiet atmosphere. There should be no sound at all, not even your favorite song. Some people recommend that you play a catchy song as you work. However, the sounds make it difficult to have an internal dialogue. If you really need to have some background music, go for instrumental pieces or environmental music.

The ideal time to tidy up your place is early in the morning after a good night's sleep (i.e. 6:30 am to 9am). During this time period, you should have the required energy and focus. The fresh air you can enjoy during that period also helps.

What to do when you can't throw something away

There are two types of judgment: rational and intuitive. It is your rational judgment that prevents you from discarding useless items. Your intuition often tells you that you no longer need an object, but your reason has the tendency to formulate various arguments against throwing it away. These thoughts will force your decision process to go back and forth.

Hesitation is not always wrong. If you can't make a quick decision, that means you are dealing with something important to you. In addition, you can't make decisions based exclusively on your intuition. A careful evaluation of each object is recommended.

When you can't decide whether to keep or discard an item, identify the reason why you own it. What were its meaning and purpose when you acquired it? Reevaluate its role in your current life.

Everything has a specific purpose. Some things need to be used until they are worn out. Others just need to be used once. When an object had served its purpose, it is time to discard it.

III. Tidying by category works like magic

Tidying order: Follow the correct order of categories

People assume that tidying up their place is full of challenges. They worry about rebound, lack of time, lack of significant benefits, etc. But their fears are usually unfounded. Here is a fact that you should remember: organizing your things is fun. It helps you understand how you feel about your possessions, identify the items that are no longer useful, express your thankfulness, and say goodbye to them; it is all about knowing your true self.

You will use your own judgment in choosing what items to keep or discard. Thus, you don't have to memorize complex formulas or theories. You just have to do the process step-by-step. Get some bags to place your garbage in and have fun.

As previously mentioned, the best order of tidying is clothes, books, papers, miscellaneous items (also known as *komono*), and things that are personally important to you (mementos). If you follow this order, you will be able to finish the task quickly and easily. You will gain momentum by discarding the unimportant stuff first. And by the time you reach the difficult items, you will have a developed process of evaluation.

You can divide each category into multiple subcategories. Let's start with clothing:

1. Tops (e.g. sweaters)
2. Bottoms (e.g. skirts)
3. Clothes you need to hang (e.g. suits)
4. Socks
5. Bags
6. Underwear
7. Accessories (e.g. hats)
8. Clothes for special events (e.g. kimonos, gowns, etc.)
9. Shoes

Dividing categories into subcategories helps you keep the process organized. You won't go back and forth between different types of items.

Important Note: The next few sections will teach you what to do with each item category.

Clothing: Place every item of clothing in the house on the floor

Get all the pieces of clothing inside your house and put them in one place. Don't proceed to the next step until you're 100% sure that you have all the clothes. Take this task seriously. Do it as if you'll have to discard all the pieces of clothing that you'll fail to find. Then divide the items into their respective categories. There should be a pile for tops, another for socks, etc.

Once you're done, some of the piles should be knee-deep. The "tops" subcategory alone should have at least 160 items. Note that this subcategory covers clothes for all seasons (e.g. shirts and sweaters). If the amount of items is intimidating, you may work on the off-season clothes first. These items are the easiest to evaluate and discard.

Answer the following questions as you evaluate each piece of clothing:

- Do you want to wear it again later?
- Would you wear it if there is a sudden change in temperature?
- Do you like to see that item again?

If your answer to any of these questions is "no", put the item in your donate or discard pile.

Loungewear: Downgrading to "loungewear" is taboo

It's difficult to discard an item that you can still use, particularly if you recently purchased it. In these situations, people keep pieces of clothing as "loungewear". They will keep the clothes even though they will never wear them in public. Downgrading a piece of clothing to loungewear doesn't work. It's likely that you will never wear the clothes you'll save this way.

Thus, you will simply fail in properly tidying up your place.

The loungewear collections of most people lay dormant for a long time. If you will ask them why they don't wear those clothes, they will tell you: "Wearing them inside the house feels wasteful," "I don't feel relaxed when I wear them," "I don't like them," etc. In other words, they use the loungewear category to delay the act of parting with unnecessary clothing.

Clothing storage: Fold it right and solve your storage problems

At this point, the clothes in your place should be down by at least 50%. The clothes you want to keep are still on the floor, waiting for you to store them away. Thus, it is the perfect time to discuss proper storage for clothes.

You have two main choices when storing a piece of clothing: fold it or put it on a hanger. Many people prefer the second option because it is quick and easy. But when tidying up your place, it is best to fold your clothes. Consider it as your primary storage method for pieces of clothing. If you think that folding requires too much work and doesn't offer many benefits, you're wrong.

Folding is 100% better than hanging. Although it greatly depends on the clothes' thickness, you can store twenty or more folded clothes in a place that can store ten hung items. Solving problems regarding clothing storage is as easy as folding your clothes.

How to fold: The best way to fold for perfect appearance

Here's a step-by-step process for folding clothes properly:

1. Visualize the would-be appearance of your storage places (e.g. drawers) once you are done.
2. Fold each garment into a smooth and simple rectangle. To do this, you should:
   a. Fold the lengthwise sides of the clothing so that they point to the center.
   b. Complete the rectangle by folding the sleeves.
   c. Fold the rectangle again so that the short ends touch each other.
   d. Do this again in thirds or halves. Adjust the folds so that your garment is of the same height as the drawer.
3. Store clothes upright. This is the best way to store clothes using minimal space. Mimicking how stores display clothes (e.g. clothes placed on top of another) leads to wasted space.

Important Note: Soft clothes are easier to fold than harder ones. You can reduce their height and width easily.

Arranging clothes: The secret to energizing your closet

It would be great if your closet contains clothes that are properly arranged. Unfortunately, this is rarely the case. Many people are scared of opening their own closets. And once they find the courage, they just can't find the specific item they are looking for.

This problem occurs because of two reasons:

1. The closet contains too many clothes
2. The person doesn't know how to organize their clothes.

You can significantly expand the space in your closet by simply folding your clothes. Don't hang a piece of clothing if you can fold it. However, there are certain clothes (e.g. suits, dresses, jackets, etc.) that require hanging. Here's a principle that you can follow: if a piece of clothing looks like it should be hung, hang it.

Now, let's address the owner's lack of knowledge. The simplest way to organize hung clothes is by dividing them into different groups (suits, dresses, jackets). Then hang clothes that belong to the same group next to each other. This rule can change the look of your closet drastically.

Storing socks: Treat your socks and stockings with respect

Your socks take punishments whenever you wear them. They are pressed between your feet and your shoes for many hours. The only time they can rest is when they are inside your drawers. And the statement is also true for your stockings. Unfortunately, they cannot rest well if they are tied, folded, or balled up. That's because their fabric is still stretched. If you'll leave them like that for a long time, they will lose their elasticity.

Let's work on your stocks first. Unfold their top sections if necessary. Put a sack on top of its pair and fold them using the technique described earlier. If your socks are low-cut, you can just fold it twice. Fold three times if you are working on ankle socks. Longer socks require four folds or more. Your main goal is to create a smooth rectangle.

Seasonal clothes: Eliminate the need to store off-season clothes

Many years ago, the changes between seasons forced people to organize their clothes accordingly. For example, when summer starts, people had to bring out their summer clothes and pack away the winter ones. Fortunately, this is no longer necessary. The advances in technology (e.g. heating and air-conditioning units) let you wear thin clothes indoors during winter. That means you can just ignore the seasons when tidying up your closets.

This approach works because it lets you know exactly the clothes you have. You don't have to implement complex methods or strategies. Basically, you will organize the clothes without pulling away the off-season ones. Don't over categorize. Use rough descriptions (e.g. wool-like or cotton-like) when classifying pieces of clothes. Basing the categories on activities or seasons is unnecessary and ineffective.

Storing books: Put all your books on the floor

Work on your books once you are done with the clothes. Note that many people find it hard to throw away books. They just can't let go of their books, even if they don't read said materials. The problem is in the approach they use during the disposal.

The first thing you have to do is put all the books on the floor. It is tempting to choose unnecessary books while they are on the shelves, but it doesn't work. You have to hold each book closely before deciding whether it should stay or go. This way, you can easily determine the importance of the book in your life. Obviously, you have to discard all the unnecessary books.

Important Note: If you have many books, you can divide them into four categories: (1) general – the books you read for pleasure, (2) practical – self-help, cookbooks, etc., (3) visual – collections of photos or illustrations, and (4) magazines.

Unread books: "Sometime" means "never"

The main reason for keeping books is that you might read them again in the future. This is a valid reason. But how many books did you actually read two or more times? If you are an author or a scientist, you'll read specific books multiple times. If you are like most people, however, you won't reread your books. Identify the purpose that they serve, if any. If they are of no use, go ahead and discard them.

There is a reason why you bought your books. You wanted to know their contents; to learn from them. If you have never opened a book for years, however, it is the perfect time to let go. Instead of keeping books you don't need, get the ones that can actually help you.

Books to keep: Those that belong in the hall of fame

You may set up your own "Hall of Fame" for books. This is a list of the books that you can't live without. For example, it may contain the fictional books that inspire and/or entertain you the most. Use this list as the basis of the books that you really need to keep.

Then, identify the books you think are important but cannot be classified as a "hall of famer". These are the books you would like to keep for now. You will find that this list will change as time passes.

Then work on the books that had a moderate effect on you. These are the books that contain moving statements. They are hard to discard because they give you some benefits. You can reduce your book collection by copying the statements you like. Record these statements in a separate notebook so that you can read them whenever you want. Then, go ahead and discard the books you took the statements from.

Sorting papers: Rule of thumb— discard everything

The paper category includes letters, invitations, flyers, newspapers, and similar files. In general, you can find pieces of paper on your bedroom table, the door of the fridge, near the phone, etc. It does not include papers with sentimental value like diaries or old love letters. Limit yourself at first to sorting the papers that give you no thrill at all and finish the job in one go. Letters from lovers or friends should be left for when you tackle sentimental items.

People assume that an office has more papers than a house. However, this is not always true. If you'll collect all the unnecessary papers in your home, you will surely fill two or more bags. When tidying up papers, you have to divide them into three types:

- Still in use
- Should be stored indefinitely
- Needed for now

Dispose all of the papers that don't belong to any of these categories. Then, divide the documents you'll keep into subcategories based on how often you'll use them. There should be two categories here: frequently used and infrequently used.

Finally, keep papers in a specific and easily accessible area of your home. Do not let them scatter to different locations.

All about papers: How to organize troublesome papers

It would be great if you can just throw away all your papers. Unfortunately, there are some papers that you can't just discard. In this chapter you'll discover the most common types of "difficult papers" and how to deal with them.

Manuals and Warranties

First, separate the appliance manuals from the warranty itself. It's unlikely that you will consult the manual in the future anyway. These manuals are often bulky, so go ahead and discard them. If you experience problems with your gadget or machine, you can use online resources to find the solution.

Then put all your warranties inside a single location. Don't separate them according to categories. In general, warranties are rarely used. Don't waste your time organizing documents that you might not even use.

Pay Slips

Pay slips show you the money you earned. After determining your income, discard the pay slips immediately.

Greeting Cards

A greeting card loses its purpose once you have received and read it. Don't let them pile up in your room. Discard these cards, except the ones that give you happiness.

Credit Card Statements

The main purpose of a credit card statement is to show your expenses. Once you have checked that information, the statement is no longer useful. Curiously, many people hoard their card statements, thinking they might need it someday (e.g. in a court hearing). But that kind of event is unlikely. And you can just ask your bank for such type of information in case you really need it. Therefore, you're free to discard every credit card statement you have already checked.

Lecture Materials

You'll get these materials from courses and seminars. Their main purpose is to help you understand the different aspects of the courses and/or seminars that you attended. However, be prepared to part ways with them once the seminar/course is over.

Komono (miscellaneous items): Keep things because you love them—not "just because"

"Komono" is the Japanese word for "miscellaneous items". Most people have these items. For example, you might have a box that contains things (e.g. erasers, loose change, key rings, etc.) that you decided to keep for some reason. This wide and vague category includes items that you don't really need. Thus, you have to discard them sooner or later.

Sort your komono in the following order:

1. CDs and DVDs
2. Makeup and other skin-related products
3. Accessories
4. Valuables (e.g. passports, credit cards, etc.)
5. Electric gadgets
6. Household equipment (e.g. stationaries, sewing kits, writing materials, etc.)
7. Household Supplies (e.g. tissues, medicine, detergents, etc.)
8. Kitchen goods/food supplies
9. Others (e.g. toys, figurines, key rings, etc.)

(If you have many items related to a particular hobby or interest, such as ski equipment or tea ceremony utensils, treat these as a single subcategory.)

This particular order is recommended because it is easier to start with more personal items and clearly defined content first. Take stock of your *komono* and save only the ones that bring you joy.

Common types of *komono:*
Disposables

There are things that you can readily identify as disposable - you know that you can throw it away as soon as you look at them. Here are the most common types of disposables that you might encounter:

- Gifts: These are the items that you received from other people. Their main purpose is to convey the sender's feelings. They attain their purpose as soon as you receive them. Thus, you don't have to feel guilty when discarding gifts you have never used.

- Spare Bedding: These items require a lot of space. Don't store many bedding sets if you rarely have guests.

- The Packaging of Electronic Gadgets: One you remove a gadget from its packaging, throw the box away.

- Broken Appliances: Send these items to a recycler in your local area.

- Cosmetic Samples: People store these items in case they go on a trip. Unfortunately, they can pile up quickly. In addition, many cosmetic samples deteriorate in just a few months. Throw these items away, unless you want to risk applying outdated cosmetics during your travels.

- Unidentified Cords: Throw away a cord if you can't identify its purpose. Almost all unidentified cords are never used. Buying one when you need it is more practical than keeping loads of them in your drawer.

- Spare Buttons: It's unlikely that you will use extra buttons. If buttons fall off, that means a piece of clothing needs to be "retired". If you really need to replace a missing button, buy one from a handicrafts shop.

- Freebies: The free pens, fans, paper cups, and similar items that you received from certain events are useless. Discard them immediately.

Small change: Make "into my wallet" your motto

You will find coins in different parts of your house. They are "real money", even if they have low value. Don't let them scatter inside your home where they become completely useless.

Put coins in your wallet whenever you see them. This way, you will be able to use them and keep your place tidy. Putting them in a piggy bank is like giving yourself a chance to ignore them.

Sentimental items: Your parents' home is not a haven for mementos

Work on this category last because it is the most difficult. An item with a sentimental value reminds you of something (e.g. a person or achievement) that brought you joy. You can't discard it because you are afraid that the precious memories attached to it will vanish. However, this belief is wrong. Your memories will stay even if you throw away every object that is related to it.

You live in the now. And you are preparing for the future. So stop focusing on the past. Find the things that give you happiness today, and keep only those.

Photos: Cherish who you are now

As you tidy up your place, you will surely find various photographs. You will find these items in different areas of the house. And sorting paragraphs as soon as you see them can be time-consuming. It would be better if you'd just collect them in a predetermined spot and deal with them in one go.

Note that you also need to sort the photos inside your albums. Empty your albums and touch the photographs one by one. Because photos exist to help you remember specific time or events, choose the ones that give you joy and keep them. Then, discard the remaining photographs.

Astounding stockpiles I have seen

Many people store large amounts of ordinary items. They fear that they might run out of something just when they need it. The items involved here vary from one household to another. Some people hoard toothbrushes or cotton swabs, while others focus on plastic kitchen wrap. Regardless of the item in question, anything in excess is bad for your home's tidiness.

If you have your own stockpile, you have to eliminate it as soon as possible. Try to use them all up. If that will take a long time, you may donate them to other people. It might sound like you are wasting money, but the freedom that you'll experience is worth it. Next time, make sure that you will limit your stocks to the right amount.

Reduce until you reach the point where something clicks

There are no specific limits when it comes to possessions. The right amount differs from one person to another. If you are living in a developed country, you likely have easy access to the things you need. Because of this, you'll have a hard time determining how much you really need to survive. Fortunately, tidying can help you with this.

As you discard stuff, you will experience an "aha" moment. You will suddenly realize the sufficient amount of possessions for you. Once it happens, you will be able to avoid excess objects naturally. Therefore, you should be safe from potential rebounds.

Follow your intuition and all will be well

You might have noticed that this method of tidying relies on your feelings and intuition. Keeping things that make you happy, hanging clothes you think must be hung, knowing the right amount of stuff you need, etc. These criteria make the method relevant to your needs and personality. They also protect you from rebounds.

Your intuition can help you greatly in tidying up your home. Always believe what your heart tells you when you ask, "Does this spark joy?" If you act on that intuition, the process of tidying up seem like magic - putting your house in order is the magic that creates a happy and vibrant life, free of unnecessary burdens and distractions.

IV. Storing your things to make your life shine

Designate a place for each thing

Set a specific location for each of your possessions. Once you do this, maintaining the tidiness of your home will be easy and natural. You will be able to keep everything organized, even if you are busy, tired, or lazy.

Note that this task requires you to assign a place for every item. You might feel that it is hard and time-consuming. However, that is not quite true. In fact, it is way much easier than choosing whether to keep or discard your items. Because you have reduced your possessions and divided them into categories, you just have to find the right areas for them.

This is an important part of the tidying method. If your items don't have a specific "home", they will end up in different parts of your house. When it happens with multiple items, clutter will come back to your life.

Important Note: Failing to assign a place for every item is the main reason why many people experience rebound. These people don't know exactly where to return the items they use, so they just store them in random locations.

Discard first, store later

Once you have discarded all the unnecessary items, the new look of your home will surprise you. The rooms will look empty. To take this step further, you may also make your bookcases disappear. Don't worry because you won't throw away your books. You just have to place the bookcases inside a cupboard or closet. This practice is an important aspect of tidying up your place.

If the closets and cupboards in your home are full, you probably think that they can no longer hold the bookcases. This is a common belief among people who are new to the art of tidying. However, it is completely wrong. There is still space that you can use. Plenty of space.

Your room has enough space to hold all your items. Many people claim that they lack space, but it is extremely rare for a room to have insufficient storage space. If you discarded everything you don't need, there will be plenty of space in your home. Thus, maximizing the storage capacity of your place is all about choosing the items to keep. This is easy to understand. If you will keep on storing unnecessary stuff, you will run out of space regardless of how huge your house is.

Storage: pursue ultimate simplicity

When it comes to tidying up your place, you have to keep things simple. Avoid complicated plans or approaches. Remember that clever ideas are not always practical. They were designed simply to boost the ego of their creator.

Instead of decoding complicated plans, identify the root cause of your clutter problem. Most people realize that clutter is generally caused by too much stuff. But why do we end up having too much stuff? Usually it is because fail to realize how much we actually own. And we fail to realize how much we own because our storage methods are unnecessarily complex. The ability to avoid excess stock depends on the capacity to simplify storage. The secret to maintaining an uncluttered home is to pursue ultimate simplicity in storage so that you can tell at a glance how much you already have.

Don't scatter storage spaces

This chapter will arm you with two important principles:

- Store items that belong to the same category together
- Don't mix up storage spaces

When it comes to belongings, there are only two methods of categorization: by owner and by item type. These categories work regardless of how many people are living in a house. If there is only one person in a house, storage is straightforward. You just have to assign a specific location for each item type. In fact, you may use the categories you used during the sorting stage to simplify the procedure.

If you are living with other people, however, things are not so easy. Aside from sorting the items, you also need to specify the storage space for every person in your home, as long as they allow you to do so. This is a crucial step of the process. For instance, you need to assign a storage space for your spouse, your children, your parents, etc. Each person must have his own space for storing things. And make sure that nobody will store items outside of his designated area. This way, you can keep the tidiness of your entire house.

In addition, having a storage space is like getting your personal sanctuary. The assigned space will be important to its owner. Because that is the only place where he can store his stuff, he is likely to keep it organized.

Forget about "flow planning" and "frequency of use"

Many people make the mistake of choosing a storage location based on convenience. If they can take an item out easily if it is placed in a particular location, then the item must be stored there. However, this approach leads to significant risks. It encourages you to store an item in a place where it doesn't really belong. Thus, the chances of rebound will increase.

Clutter occurs because a person doesn't return objects to their proper location. Thus, the ease of putting items away should be the top priority when choosing a storage location. Don't worry about the effort needed to take the items out. When you are looking for an item, you probably have a definite purpose for it. That means you are willing to spend some time and effort to get the item you need.

The design of your home can serve as a guide. If you analyze the different parts of your house, you will identify the best storage areas for your stuff.

Important Note: When deciding whether to keep an item or not, let your heart guide you. When it comes to choosing storage spaces, however, let your house "decide".

Never pile things: vertical storage is the key

There are people who organize things by putting one item on top of another. This is a common approach, but it is wrong. Piling things leads to wasted space. It is always better to store your possessions vertically. If you follow this rule religiously, you will be able to save a surprising amount of storage space.

Use vertical arrangement whenever possible. This approach works best for clothes, boxes, erasers, and similar objects. You may even store laptops vertically. If your storage space is insufficient, try storing the items vertically. You'll find that this simple adjustment can solve most of your storage problems.

Important Note: Piling things can negatively affect the bottommost objects. For example, clothes at the bottom of a pile may get squished so much that their fabrics are ruined. Documents, meanwhile, are easy to forget about when there are many papers on top of them.

No need for commercial storage items

There are many types of storage items available on the market. They have interesting features such as cloth racks and movable dividers. And you can get them from both local and online stores. Interestingly, you don't really need any of them.

Instead of spending your hard-earned money on these pricey "solutions", go for cheaper ones instead. For example, you may use plastic drawers for your clothes and miscellaneous items. Place your small items in cardboard drawers. Then put your towels in baskets. Then you can store these in a closet. You can eliminate the need for bookcases by putting your books inside a cupboard. As you can see, these simple storage devices can do the trick. They don't cost much, but they can certainly protect your items.

If you want multi-purpose containers, you may use empty shoe boxes. They can hold different types of objects. And they are completely free. These boxes are great because they are durable and easy to use. Since most shoe boxes have cute designs, they can also be attractive. You may use a shoebox for storing socks and stockings. In the bathroom, you can use it to hold shampoo and conditioner bottles.

You may also use the lids of the shoeboxes as trays. They can keep the cupboard's base clean by holding materials such as spices and cooking oils. Unlike most shelf liners, the lid of a shoebox is easy to replace and discard.

The best way to store bags is in another bag

Bags are difficult to store because they occupy too much space. You can't fold them since they will lose their shape. To solve this problem, people usually fill their bags with tissue paper (e.g. to retain their shape) and hang them (usually in prime locations). But this approach has two main disadvantages. First, the tissue paper adds to the unnecessary objects in your house. Second, the bags greatly reduce the space available to other items.

Fortunately, a powerful solution exists. This solution allows you to save space and maintain the shape of each bag. All you have to do is place a bag inside another bag. To get the most out of this solution, however, you should divide your bags into different categories (e.g. soft, stiff, thin, thick, etc.). Then, put a small bag inside a bigger one that belongs to the same category. Each bag can hold up to two smaller bags.

Empty your bag every day

Some items (e.g. wallet, datebook) have to be inside your bag every day. If you're like most people, you don't remove these things from your bag in order to save time and effort. Why would you take them out if you'll use them again tomorrow? It turns out that leaving your stuff inside your bag is a huge mistake.

Your bag's job is to hold your item while you are outside the house. If you won't let it rest (i.e. by emptying it), it will look worn and tired. It will immediately lose its shape and beauty. In addition, you'll have a hard time remembering the exact contents of your bags if you will not inspect them every day.

Empty your bags daily. Don't worry - you are not going to waste a lot of time and energy on this task. Place the bags' contents in an empty box. Then arrange those items vertically. The items are necessary so you have to store them in a place you can easily access. For example, you may put the box on top of a large container. If the location of the box is near the storage spot for your bags, that's even better.

Items that usurp floor space belong in the closet

A built-in closet is a great storage space. It can hold most of your belongings. You can get the most out of your built-in closets by following these tips:

- Store off-season items (e.g. winter decorations, skiwear) above your closet. This spot is also great for large objects with sentimental value.
- Place your clothes inside the closet. Organize them vertically to save space.
- The upper part of closets is ideal for beddings. That spot offers excellent protection against dust and humidity.
- Use the bottom of the closet to store electrical appliances (e.g. fans during winter, space heaters during summer).

Keep things out of the bath and the kitchen sink

Bathrooms are almost always wet and humid. They are also prone to slimy problems, thanks to the bottles of shampoos and conditioners inside them. Because of these reasons, it is a bad idea to store anything inside a bathroom.

Don't put your shampoo bottles and soap bars inside your bathroom if you are not using them. The moisture and temperature in the bathroom can ruin their quality. Thus, it is best to dry the said items after you use them, and then store them in a cupboard. Although it sounds like extra work, it actually simplifies your cleaning tasks. Your bathroom will be free from clutter, which means it is easier to clean. The chances of slime buildup are also lower.

The statements given above also apply to your kitchen sink. Store your sponges and detergents under the kitchen sink. Before storing them, however, make sure that they are completely dry. Instead of leaving them by the kitchen sink, hang your sponges outside the house (e.g. the veranda).

Make the top shelf of the bookcase your personal shrine

If you have special objects such as good-luck charms or protective talismans, you should organize them too. Having too much of these objects can lead to clutter. You should also note that these items have expiration dates. For instance, a Buddhist charm is effective only for one year after you receive it. After that time, the charm should be returned to a Buddhist temple. Conversely, if you practice Shintoism, you have to return the said objects to a shrine. The point here is that you should get rid of charms and talismans as soon as they expire.

Now that you have trimmed your talisman collection, it's time to set up your own altar. Choose an area in your room (e.g. the top shelf of the bookcase) and put all your active talismans on it. Your simple altar and tidy living space will fill you with the pure energy that you need.

Decorate your closet with your secret delights

Many people have items they don't want others to see. Their owners are not comfortable displaying them in public. Posters of pop idols or hobby-related books are excellent representatives for this category.

If you have this kind of item, don't hide it in a drawer. It plays an important part in your life. It gives you joy. And your room should allow you to show the real you. Instead of placing your beloved item in a dark corner of your room, put it inside your closet. Consider your closet as the repository of everything that is special to you. This way, your closet will be a private are - it will give you pleasure whenever you open it. You may use your special items as decorations for the closet's door or back wall.

Important Note: Your closet is your most private storage space. Decorate it as much as you want. Use it to present your special possessions in a way that inspires you.

Unpack and de-tag new clothes immediately

Buying a lot of clothes in one go seems convenient. It lets you save time and effort. People who stockpile clothes usually leave the items in their original packages. This approach lets you store clothes straight from the shopping bag. However, it leads to wasted space.

Stockpiling clothes is not as economical as you might think. You'll have to keep an item that you don't need yet. In addition, an item might lose its beauty while it is biding its time at the bottom of your drawer. For these reasons, it is best to buy clothes just when you need them.

And don't store clothes without removing their tags and packages. The unnecessary materials that come with new products will just consume space. Throw these materials away as soon as you can.

Don't underestimate the "noise" of written information

Written information has a significant effect on tidiness. You can discard and organize things all you want, but your room will still feel "stuffed" if it contains many written messages. A common example for this is the labels of storage solutions you might be using. These pieces of information, when combined, can create distracting "noises".

Visual information can affect you in many ways. If your closet contains many written materials, for example, just the simple act of choosing clothes to wear can be pretty taxing. If you want to enjoy your living space, eliminate all the unnecessary information present in it.

Appreciate your possessions and gain strong allies

Your belongings play an important role in your life. They help you 24/7. Thus, you should appreciate them for all the good things they are doing for you. It is a simple task. You just have to talk to your belongings as if they are human beings. Here are some statements that you can use:

- "Thanks for helping me do my job."
- "Thanks for protecting me from the cold."
- "Thanks for improving how I look."

This technique will enhance your appreciation for your possessions. If you will do this regularly, your relationship with your items and your living space will be more intimate.

This technique will enhance the lifespan of almost all items. This is easy to understand. If you will explicitly show your appreciation for an object, you will take good care of it. Thus, it will exceed its natural lifespan.

Important Note: If you treat your items well, they will serve you for a long period of time. If you use them carelessly, however, you will constantly find yourself buying large amounts of the same stuff.

V. The magic of tidying dramatically transforms your life

Put your house in order and discover what you really want to do

The things you love to do revealed themselves to you when you were young. If you don't know what you would like to do now, look back to your primary and high school days. Those periods of your life have clues regarding your true passions. And tidying up your house can help you greatly.

When you organize your stuff, you'll know the things you hold dear. The books you thought were important might no longer interest you. The miscellaneous items you hid, meanwhile, might start to communicate with you in a special way. These events can encourage people to change jobs, do volunteer work, get married, etc. You have a deep connection with the things you decided to keep. And they can tell you many things about yourself that you haven't figured out yet.

The magic effect of tidying

Discarding can be more powerful than obtaining new stuff. When you throw away an object, you free up space for something more important. You also reduce the number of items that require your time and/or attention.

If there are hundreds of books you are planning to read, for instance, you have a difficult time ahead of you. Even if you succeed in reading all of those books, you can't be sure that you'll remember their most important lessons. But you can take a different approach. Reduce this list to the "bare essentials". Focus on the books that teach you what you really need to know. You will be surprised at how fast you'll acquire various types of information.

This principle applies to many things. And it can significantly alter your life. Specifically, discarding helps you in improving your ability to make decisions. In addition, it encourages you to implement your decisions as soon as you can.

Important Note: Tidying up your room is not just about improving your living space. It can also improve your confidence and decision-making skills.

Gaining confidence in life through the magic of tidying

Tidying up your room is a great way to develop your confidence. This activity requires you to work alone, make decisions, take actions, form plans, and other challenging tasks. Once you are done, your living space will match the way you want to live your life. You will also create a powerful connection with everything that you own.

If you are comfortable with the clothes you wear, the items you use, and the place you live in, you will be more confident with your environment. You will find that interacting with other people, even those with a higher position than you, will be easy. The process of organizing your things forces you to know yourself. It is a powerful form of introspection. If done correctly, it can help you identify your own strengths, weaknesses, fears, and aspirations.

An attachment to the past or anxiety about the future

Once you get used to discarding unnecessary things, you will be able to identify the importance of an object just by touching it.

At first, your mind will come up with countless reasons for keeping a useless item. But if you are sure that you don't need it, you have to overcome your mind's objections. This kind of objection is either a result of fear or attachment.

When you find yourself unable to discard an unimportant item, identify the cause of the problem. Do you want to keep it because you are afraid of what might happen in the future? Or is it because of your attachment to past events? These questions will help you see your "ownership pattern" (i.e. the pattern you follow regarding your possessions). There are three types of ownership patterns: (1) desire for stability in the future, (2) attachment to the past, and (3) a combination of both.

You should know your ownership pattern because it reflects your personal values. Your remaining possessions reflect the lifestyle you want to achieve. Your fears regarding the future and/or attachment to past events are not limited to the things you currently own. To some extent, they also affect your career, the decisions you make every day, and your personal relationships.

There are certain mindsets that stop people from maximizing their potential. First, a person might choose something because it seems advantageous even if he doesn't really like it. Second, he might choose something just for security reasons. He thinks he might end up missing an opportunity if he won't make the acquisition. Third, he might avoid obtaining new items because of his attachment to his old possessions. Lastly, he doesn't want to try new stuff in new situations because their old items worked in the past.

When these mindsets stop you from discarding things, you won't know your current needs. You will have a hard time identifying the things you really want, and the amount of your belongings will increase. Acquiring stuff like this is like burying yourself in unnecessary objects. It affects you mentally and physically. Fortunately, you can determine the things you need by discarding what you don't.

Analyzing and choosing your belongings can be quite difficult. It requires you to face your mistakes and weaknesses. It forces you to examine the wrong decisions you made before. But this is an important part of personal growth. You have to correct your mistakes. If you ignore them, you will make the same errors over and over again.

There are three approaches that you can take toward your possessions: face them now, face them some other time, or forget about them. The best choice is to face them now. If you acknowledge your attachment to the past and your fears for the future by honestly looking at your possessions, you will be able to see what is really important to you. This process in turn helps you identify your values and reduces doubt or confusion in making life decisions. If you're confident in your decisions and jump into action without any doubts holding you back, you will be able to achieve much more. In other words, the sooner you confront your possessions the better. If you are going to put your house in order, do it now.

Learning that you can do without

People who take tidying up seriously end up disposing of many garbage backs. Curiously, these people don't experience any inconvenience despite the huge decrease of their possessions. They usually don't complain about items they wish to get back. This is easy to understand: they didn't discard anything important. They carefully examine everything before deciding what to throw away. Thus, they don't feel any adverse effect on their lifestyle. This statement holds true for everyone. You will most likely feel that you have everything you need even after throwing away about 80% of your current belongings.

It doesn't mean that you won't regret discarding your stuff. You will have this kind of feeling multiple times while tidying up your place. But you shouldn't allow it to stop you. Once regret goes away, you'll discover that you can definitely survive without the things you put in the trash bin.

There's a chance that you will need something (e.g. a document) that you discarded before. This is not good, but it is not as bad as you think. Because you removed all the clutter, you can easily confirm that you don't have the item anymore. That means you can move on to other solutions. Having the item buried in tons of clutter, on the other hand, doesn't really help. You would have to spend a lot time searching for that particular item. And if you have lots of unnecessary stuff, you might never find the important item again. Clearly, it is better to know that you have lost it than tell yourself that "it is there somewhere".

In addition, discarding things force you to take responsibility. You will make your own decisions and stand by them. Since you are the person who threw away your things, you cannot blame others. People who tidy their own living spaces tend to have more confidence in making important decisions.

Do you greet your house?

You take good care of your gadgets. You appreciate your clothes. Thus, it is also necessary that you consider the role your house plays in your life.

Greet your house when you arrive. Talk to it as if it is another human being. If you are embarrassed, you don't have to say the words aloud. This simple technique will help you develop a relationship not just with the things you own, but also with the place you live in. Your home keeps you and your possessions safe. And it is just right that you appreciate its work.

Once you've done this for a while, you will feel a significant change in your home. You'll feel as if your dwelling responds to you whenever you arrive. The mere act of going through the door will give you pleasure. In addition, your house will "show" you the ideal storage locations for your stuff. You will just know where to put what once you get genuinely attached to your home.

Your possessions want to help you

People differ in terms of the way they organize their stuff. No two individuals share the same exact system for tidying up. However, every object that is currently owned shares one particular characteristic: it wants to help its owner as much as it can. You acquired an item because you want to use it. But you should also consider the fact that the item is created to help its owner (i.e. you). This statement applies to every object that you possess.

You have a deep connection with the things you own. Let's consider the shirt you are wearing, for instance. The manufacturer produced hundreds or thousands of those shirts in its factory. But the shirt that you paid for and brought home is unique. It is your shirt, and that makes it special. There are many other objects in this world, but your belongings found their way to your home. In a way, they are similar to the people you will meet in your life. There are billions of people out there. But only a few of them will meet you and stay with you.

Since every object you own wants to assist you, it is just fitting that you say goodbye to them before discarding them. Thank them for their services. Appreciate their work before letting them go.

Your living space affects your body

Many people experience positive changes in their body while decluttering their living space. Some lose weight while others obtain firmer muscles. This is difficult to explain. For some reason, detoxifying your home can help you in detoxifying your own body.

Discarding large amounts of stuff can affect the hormones and toxins present in your body. You might suffer from acne breakouts and/or diarrhea. If you experience any of these, don't panic. Your body is just eliminating the toxins inside it. In 24 to 48 hours, your body should return to normal.

By removing the clutter in your house, you can greatly improve your health. The amount of dust in your living space will decrease. The air you breathe will become fresher and cleaner. Because your house is organized, you will be able to relax and sleep easily. And because you don't have to worry about maintaining large amounts of stuff, you'll have more time to focus on yourself and on those things that truly deserve your attention.

Is it true that tidying increases good fortune?

Feng Shui, a method of organizing your surrounding environment to boost luck, is highly popular in different parts of the globe. Consequently, many people want to know whether the art of tidying can really make someone lucky. There are also some individuals who want to sort out their things for the sole purpose of attracting good fortune.

Well, you don't really have to believe in fortune or feng shui. But you can certainly incorporate elements of feng shui in your personal tidying system to harmonize your personal environment. When organizing your clothes, for instance, you may arrange the items by their color so that they "move" from light to dark. Put the light-colored items in front. Then place the darker clothes at the back. Note that this style of arrangement requires you to store clothes vertically.

How to identify what is truly precious

It is easy to determine whether an item is important to you or not. You don't have to do complex tasks such as estimating an object's "age". All you need to do is analyze your reaction when you hold the particular item.

When holding something that is important to you, you tend to have a contented look on your face, and you decide to keep it without hesitation. If an item is unnecessary, however, you will likely have a slightly negative facial expression. You might even frown in concentration while deciding whether to keep the item or not. In this situation, it is usually best to dispose of it.

But you can still make this kind of assessment without analyzing your own gestures and reactions. You just have to look at the items themselves. A precious item is like a person in love. It radiates happiness and the willingness to help. If you cherish it and handle it with care, the object will "shine" in front of your eyes.

Being surrounded by things that spark joy makes you happy

You surely have a belonging that you deeply love - an object that you can never discard. You intend to keep it, even if other people cannot understand your fascination. This "special something" can take many forms. It can be an old toy, a teddy bear, a collectible card, etc. Pinpointing the beautiful aspect of such items is not easy. But when you talk to their owners, you will readily know that they couldn't part with those objects.

Keep your special items no matter what. If you feel joy when you are holding an item, don't listen to people who tell you to discard it. You don't have to use or wear the item in public. Use it in ways that make you happy.

Important Note: One of the greatest forms of happiness that you can experience in this world is to have the things you love. Be contented with the things that "touch" your heart. Avoid acquiring and keeping things you don't really want or need. By doing so, you will be able to fully appreciate your beloved items.

Your real life begins after putting your house in order

Many people believe that tidying is a daily chore. They assume that it is a never-ending task. But nothing could be further from the truth. You can (and must) tidy up your place in just one go. Eliminate all the unnecessary stuff during your first (and only) major discarding session.

It is not mandatory to tidy up your living space. Nobody died because of a messy room. And millions of people don't even care about the arrangement of their possessions. However, these individuals will never touch a book such as this. You, on the other hand, are reading this book. That means you are willing to change the way you live. You want to have a new lifestyle. You want to be more focused and less distracted. You want to achieve happiness and personal growth. These desires are strong enough to motivate you to sort out all your things. The process of improving your living space began when you picked up this book. And now that you are done reading it, you know exactly what you need to do.

Do not spend too much time on this task, though. It is best to tidy up rapidly and get it over with. Why? Because tidying is probably not your main purpose in life. However, putting your house in order will help you find that purpose. Life truly begins after you finish tidying up your living space.

Millionaire Mind Book Summaries

Millionaire Mind Publishing provides the greatest self-help, productivity, and personal development books summarized for your convenience.

Our summaries aim to teach you important lessons in a time efficient and cost effective manner. They highlight key ideas and fundamental concepts found in the original books. Unessential information is removed to save the reader time.

Save time and money while completing your reading list. Get your life-changing Millionaire Mind summary right now!

https://www.amazon.com/Millionaire-Mind-Publishing/e/B01ECUVK48/

P.S. If you enjoyed this summary, please take a few minutes of your time and leave a review on Amazon.com. It will be greatly appreciated!

Thank you and good luck!